FIREHOUSE

FIREHOUSE

BY BERNARD WOLF

WILLIAM MORROW & COMPANY · NEW YORK · 1983

ACKNOWLEDGMENTS: The challenges and difficulties posed by this book could not possibly have been surmounted without the generous and patient assistance of some very special people. The author wishes particularly to thank David Reuther, Pamela D. Pollack and Sylvia Frezzolini of Morrow Junior Books; John J. Mulligan, Assistant Commissioner, Press Office, New York Fire Department; Lieutenant Frank Cull, Retired Press Officer, New York Fire Department; Battalion Chiefs John Beaulieu and Joseph G. DiBernardo, formerly the Commanding Officers of 42 Great Jones Street; and Harvey Eisner, Captain, Tenafly Volunteer Fire Department, Tenafly, New Jersey. However, words are inadequate to describe the patience, kindness, courtesy and tolerant good humor given the author over a period of months by the firefighters depicted in this book. God bless you all!

Printed in the United States of America.

1 2 3 4 5 6 7 8 9 10

Library of Congress Cataloging in Publication Data: Wolf, Bernard. Firehouse. Summary: Describes the life and work of fire fighters who operate out of a fire station on New York's Lower East Side, a neighborhood plagued by arson in recent years. 1. Fire stations—New York—Juvenile literature. 2. New York (N.Y.)—Fires and fire prevention—Juvenile literature. [1. Fire fighters. 2. Fire departments—New York (N.Y.) 3. New York (N.Y.)—Fires and fire prevention] I. Title. TH9505.N508W64 1983 363.3′78′097471 83-1174
ISBN 0-688-01734-7
ISBN 0-688-01735-5 (lib. bdg.)

For the men and officers of Engine Company 33
and Ladder Company 9, and all of the firefighters
throughout this great city who daily risk their lives on
our behalf and who are truly "New York's Bravest."

In New York City, there are two short blocks called Great Jones Street. At number 42 stands a firehouse, the home for Engine Company 33 and Tower Ladder Company 9. Engine 33 and Ladder 9 respond to alarms from roughly 6th Avenue on the west side of Manhattan to Avenue C on the east side, and from Delancey Street north to 14th Street. This area contains a large and historically interesting chunk of real estate, the heart of New York's Lower East Side. Today this area is undergoing a renaissance. While a lot of old tenement and factory warehouse buildings remain in use, many more have been converted into artists' studios and spacious lofts for the affluent. There are even some new high-rise luxury apartment buildings and brownstone town houses here and there.

But a few blocks south of 42 Great Jones Street is an area known for its cheap bars and sleazy flophouses. The farther east one goes, the more serious problems become. Over the past two decades, arson has become a fact of life here. On street after street are the devastated shells of burned-out, abandoned tenements. It looks like a war zone. For the men of Engine 33 and Ladder 9 who have fought practically every fire in the area, it has been exactly that.

The techniques of fighting fires have not changed much since the turn of the century, but the equipment certainly has. On the old brick floor of the firehouse stand two of the most sophisticated pieces of firefighting equipment devised by modern technology: the pumper and the tower ladder. On either side of the floor stand the four polished brass fire poles which rise to the inside roof of the build-

ing some eighty feet above. These provide quick access to the apparatus when an alarm comes in, and they get a lot of use. From any corner of the two floors above, a man can complete his slide down to the bottom, pull his shoes off, slip into his steel-soled and toed rubber boots, grab his lined fire coat, don his leather helmet, and climb aboard his vehicle.

Having a meal in the firehouse is not always good for the digestion. On the average of seven times out of ten, no sooner do the men on duty complete their cooking and sit down to enjoy their food, when an alarm comes in. Today is no exception. As the buzzer sounds in the kitchen, all ears are alerted to the information it carries. One buzz means that only the engine will make this run; two buzzes, only the truck; and three buzzes means that everybody goes. When the third buzz is heard, some men take an extra big bite of their tuna sandwiches, others swallow some more coffee, and they all run to get their gear. The two front doors of the house have already been raised by the man on house watch, and the mighty roar of both great machines shakes the very foundations of the building.

Before the vehicles exit, their sirens are already shrieking and there are repeated blasts from the engine's bull horn to warn cars on the street. The engine is always the first one to leave on a run. It has priority because it will supply water to fight the fire. The powerful pump, concealed within the engine's body like a giant heart, has the capacity to feed water to five hose lines at the same time. The pump can generate as much as 1,000 gallons of water per minute.

Firemen speeding through the city's streets never know what they will face when they reach their destination. But when both the truck and the engine are called to an alarm, there is greater probability of finding a serious fire. Sure enough, as they round the corner of East 9th Street, the men see a huge tower of black smoke billowing above a six-story apartment building. Other firefighting

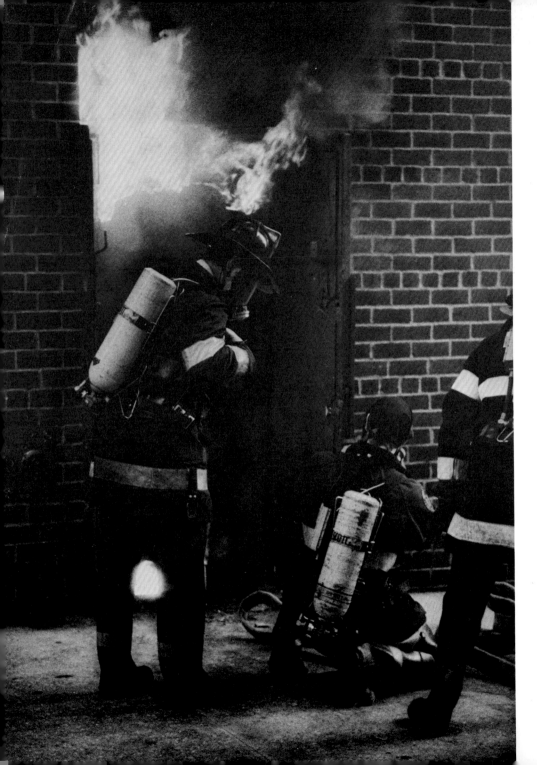

companies are already on the scene. This is an "all hands" alarm, indicating a particularly hazardous fire situation, and extra help is needed.

The fire is in the kitchen grease duct of a restaurant on the street level. Quickly, a hose line is stretched from the engine stationed at the corner. Once inside, the men discover that the fire has spread through the large kitchen and has now ignited the dining area as well. The hose is turned on and the men try to knock down or contain the fire's further advance.

There is a service door to the kitchen on the other side of the building. But it is made of heavy steel and is locked from the inside. It must be forced open. Instantly, an intense ball of flame bursts out into the faces of the men standing by. Backing away, they put on their Scott air packs.

The Scott air pack consists of a compressed air tank to which a face mask is attached by a flexible two-foot

length of air hose. The tank contains a thirty-minute air supply, *if* a man is not exerting himself; but under real working conditions, a twenty-minute supply is more realistic. The entire unit weighs about twenty-three pounds. But most firemen don't like to use Scott air packs. It isn't the weight the men object to. (Between the turnout gear he wears and the tools and equipment he has with him, each man is carrying an average of 105 pounds above his own body weight.) The problem is that the face mask severely limits a man's field of vision. In heavy smoke, the lens of the Scott mask quickly fogs over and makes visibility even worse. Because the mask shields only a man's face, sometimes his ears and neck may be badly burned before he realizes that he is too close to the fire. Nevertheless, in addition to saving lives, the Scott pack enables an engine crew to move a hose line into a smoke-filled building much more rapidly than it could without it.

Through the walkie-talkie he wears, the officer at the opened service door tells the men working inside the restaurant that his hose men are ready to activate their line. Then he asks his motor pump operator (the man who hooks up the engine's pumps to the nearest fire hydrant) to give him water. With tremendous velocity, water jets from the nozzle into the kitchen and immediately darkens the interior with a blanket of smoke. The officer makes sure that the main body of fire in front of them is thoroughly doused. Then through his face mask he yells, "Okay, let's go!" and he and his hose men charge inside, chasing the retreating wall of flame. With his crew pushing the fire in one direction, and with the hose men from the dining area pushing it in another, both teams must be careful not to force the flames into each other's path.

Meanwhile, Aerial Ladder Company 9 has raised its ladder to the top of the building. A fireman with a walkie-talkie climbs to the roof. Since heat rises most quickly in a duct or air-shaft fire, the top floor and roof of a building are the most vulnerable places. A man can climb the aerial ladder in less time than it would take to reach the roof via the hallway stairs or in an elevator that might not be working. Having made his inspection, the fireman radios to the deputy fire chief who is running this operation from the street below: In addition to the heavy black smoke, there are also sparks coming out of the grease duct where it leaves the roof of the building.

Inside, the men of Ladder 9 are methodically searching each apartment above the fire floor. Their job is to find the grease duct so they can follow its rise up through the floors and determine whether the fire is spreading to a higher level. This isn't easy, because not even the building superintendent knows where the duct is concealed.

Several apartment doors must be forced open when no one answers the doorbells. They find the duct where they least expect it—in a shaft of its own inside a wall between two bathrooms. The heat coming from this section of wall in one apartment is so great that they have no choice but to chop the wall open with their axes. The fire has escaped the duct and ignited some of the two-by-fours inside. Once they extinguish it with the portable water tanks they carry, the men must examine every apartment above this one to make certain that the fire isn't breaking out anywhere else.

Inside the restaurant, all flames have been extinguished. The nozzles of both hose lines are adjusted to the "fog" setting. This ejects a powerful spray of fine mist which vents the last traces of heat and smoke out through the kitchen door into the street. The place is a mess, but the fire is out.

A fireman's job is not completed after a fire has been extinguished. During the fire, all his senses are revved to maximum efficiency, and he is rarely aware of how hard he is driving himself. When it's over, he is dirty, sweaty and tired. He has inhaled some smoke. His mouth and throat are dry and taste awful. Maybe he is feeling a little shaky after a close call during the fire. It doesn't matter. There is a lot of work left to be done.

A pumper carries sixty lengths of hose line in three diameters; each length is fifty feet long, weighs about thirty pounds, and is constructed of rubber-lined polyester. The pumper's twenty-two lengths of 2½-inch-width hose are the most frequently used. They are more flexible than the larger 3½-inch size and provide an adequate volume of water for most fires. The 1¾-inch hose, which is even more flexible, is often used for small tenement fires, while the 3½-inch size is usually reserved for big commercial buildings where the maximum volume of water is required.

After the ladder company is finished inside the building, probing lingering hot spots with their hooks and axes, it must take up the hundreds of feet of hose line strewn on the street outside. This tedious, time-consuming but essential process is called overhauling. After unscrewing the metal coupling rings that join each length of hose, the men drain the lines of any remaining water by slinging each fifty-foot length of hose over their shoulders and pushing it away from themselves as they walk back to the engine. Then each section must be recoupled. Finally all the lines are hoisted onto the rear of the engine where they must be carefully folded back into the engine's hose bed in readiness for the next run.

When a fire-alarm box is activated and no address given, Engine 33 alone makes the run to the box location to find out what the problem is. This time, in an alleyway between two burned-out buildings, the company arrives to find an abandoned car on fire.

Putting out a car fire is relatively easy. On the bottom, near the rear of the engine chassis, a booster tank that contains 500 gallons of water is kept filled at all times. At the rear of the engine the two-inch booster line, a little wider than a garden hose, is coiled. As soon as the engine is parked, the men pull the booster line into the alley. The water in the booster tank is more than enough to put out the fire. In a few moments the fire is out. Next, the men must make sure that no embers have spread to the mounds of rubble and junk strewn everywhere. If that happened, the buildings on both sides of the alley could ignite.

The booster line is cranked back onto its reel and Engine 33 returns to the station. The entire operation has taken about fifteen minutes.

Rubbish fires are another nuisance because there are so many of them. They are set by careless pedestrians who toss burning cigarettes into trash cans, by kids looking for a little excitement, by derelicts attempting to keep warm in the winter. Engine 33's booster line can extinguish most of these fires within moments after the company arrives on the scene. But no matter how quickly they are put out, there is always the danger they may spread and ignite buildings or even parked cars.

The countless false alarms that Engine 33 responds to day in and day out are an even bigger nuisance than rubbish fires. The fire department wastes thousands of man hours each year chasing down these costly pranks. But when a street alarm box is activated, Engine 33 has to go out and take a look, even if the men feel sure that they will find nothing. There is always the possibility that this time they may discover a serious fire in progress. It's all part of their job.

In every firehouse in New York City, alarms are received at the house-watch position via teleprinter computer from a fire-department central dispatch station. The fireman assigned to house-watch duty is the eyes and ears of his house. When the alarm printout emerges from the machines, it provides the man on duty with the alarm-box number closest to the scene and the address, if known, of the building where the fire is suspected. What is frequently not supplied is the nature of the problem. Most people who call the fire department are not sure themselves of what is happening. As a result, the men at 42 Great Jones Street are seldom aware of what lies in store for them when they go out on a run. This uncertainty is a part of the tension they have learned to live with.

Late on a steamy summer afternoon both Engine 33 and Ladder 9 respond to an all-hands alarm. This time, from the alarm printout, they know that a serious fire is in progress. As the firemen rush into the burning tenement with their hose line, an elderly woman runs past them into the street. She is terrified but un-

harmed. The fire is on the fourth floor, and it is a nasty one. Dense black smoke pours out of the rear windows. Within minutes the tower ladder is raised, and the two men in the bucket move it toward the burning apartment. If people are trapped inside, they can be lowered in the bucket safely to the ground. At the same time, men from the ladder company search each apartment and evacuate the other tenants as quickly as possible.

A body is discovered in a smoke-filled room on the fire floor. A very old invalid woman is lying in her bed unconscious. There is no time to wait for the ladder. One man picks her up and runs down the four flights of stairs, carrying her over his shoulder. He deposits her on the sidewalk across the street from the building, where she is surrounded by concerned fellow tenants. "Somebody call an ambulance!" a man yells.

"She needs oxygen," pants the fireman who made the rescue, and he races

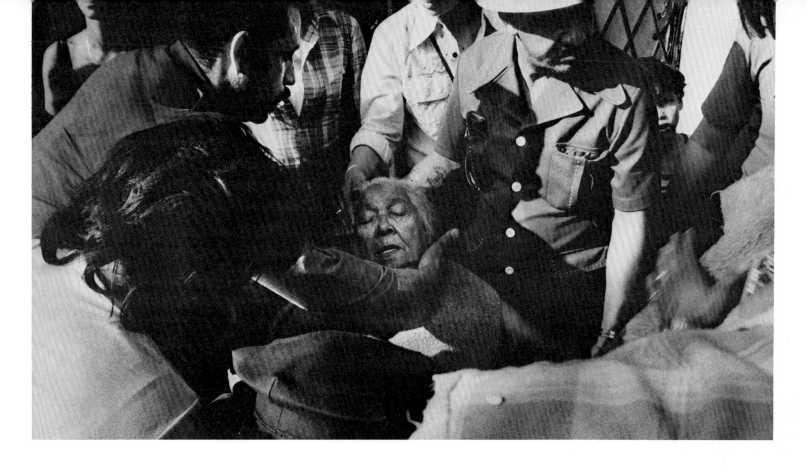

toward his truck. Moments later, he returns with a resuscitation kit. Kneeling by her side, he places the oxygen mask over her mouth and nose. She is suffering from smoke inhalation and severe shock.

By now, the engine men have water in the hose line, ready to go. At the same time, two men from the truck company have positioned themselves on the fire escape in front, ready to break the windows to expel the built-up heat and smoke inside. Timing is crucial. The engine officer in charge of the hose line inside speaks into his walkie-talkie. "All set here," he says.

This is what the vent men are waiting to hear. Using their axes, they smash in the windows and scramble down the fire escape to the landing below where they flatten themselves against the building's facade. "All set to vent!" one of them yells into his walkie-talkie. With astonishing force, an avalanche of water erupts from the interior, carrying with it bits of debris as well as a cloud of white, steamy smoke.

An ambulance has just arrived on the scene. It stops in front of the woman lying on the sidewalk. She is placed on a stretcher. Then, with the ambulance siren shrieking through the street, she is gone.

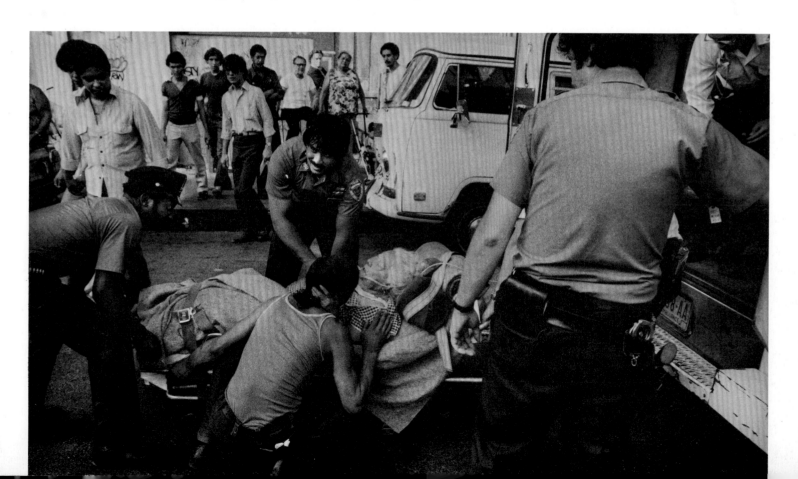

Every evening, at 6:00 P.M. exactly, roll call is taken. The night crews for both companies report for work and are given their assignments. They will be on duty a total of fifteen hours until 9:00 A.M. the following morning, when the day tour crews relieve them.

A fireman will work Monday and Tuesday from 9:00 A.M. until 6:00 P.M. He gets Wednesday off, then reports back for night tour from 6:00 P.M. until 9:00 A.M. on Thursday and Friday. He has the next three days off.

The evening meal at the firehouse is usually the highlight of the night tour. This week, it's the truck company's turn to shop for the evening meals. Inside the supermarket, Fireman Collins wears a walkie-talkie. If Ladder 9 receives an alarm, he and the other men will drop what they are doing and run for the truck. Their meal will have to wait.

"We're spending too much money for all this junk," grumbles Mo Ambrosini, as he helps the check-out clerk pack their food.

"What're you gripin' about *now*?" Jimmy Collins asks. "You never had it so good at home and you know it. Besides," he adds, "I don't notice *you* ever offering to cook a meal for us."

"That's because you jokers wouldn't know gourmet cooking even if I stuck it under your noses. So I figure, why bother? See what I mean?" retorts Mo with a grin.

Tonight's meal is meatballs and sausages in a savory tomato sauce, served over linguine, with buttered Italian garlic bread, a big mixed salad, and for dessert, two different kinds of pie.

Nick Vadola transfers the browned sausages to a large kettle and starts prepar-

ing the sauce. Nick has been a fireman for over nineteen years, most of them spent at 42 Great Jones Street. He wouldn't trade jobs with anyone in New York City. He is probably the strongest man in the house. Although he has a remarkably gentle disposition, he is seldom teased by his fellow firefighters.

"Little" Albo Nelson gets ribbed constantly because of his height. But he is a tough customer and can dish it out as well as the bigger men.

Mo just won't quit. "What makes a little squarehead like you think he can fix *Italian* meatballs?" he jeers.

Dinner is delicious. When it is over, the men clear away the debris, wash the dishes, and scrub the pots and pans. Leftovers are stored in the refrigerator for late-night snacks. For once, they have not been interrupted by an alarm.

"Not a bad deal at all," Nick Vadola comments, "considering that it only cost us two and a half bucks a man. . . ."

On Saturday mornings, multi-unit apparatus drill is conducted in the street outside of quarters. For passersby, the most impressive show is provided by the men of Ladder 9 when they put the tower ladder through its paces.

Weighing 44,700 pounds, it carries no water tanks and only a few rolled up lengths of hose to be connected directly to the pumper. On the bottom of the chassis there are four hydraulic jacks, two at the front and two behind the truck's huge rear wheels. Before the tower boom can be raised, these jacks must be activated, forcing the truck up until the entire chassis is raised two inches above the ground. Then two hydraulic outriggers drop to the ground on both sides at the center of the truck. These project out six feet, so that when the tower ladder is raised to either side above the truck, the chassis is stable. Otherwise, the enormous weight of the ladder would cause the entire rig to fall on its side, bringing the tower ladder crashing down. Even with the outriggers down, when the tower ladder is in full extension to one side of the truck, the outrigger on the other side may be raised as much as three or four inches off the ground.

The tower boom itself rests upon a revolving turntable and rises in three telescoping sections to its maximum extension of seventy-five feet. Running up its spine is a ladder which is used only in extreme emergencies. If for some reason the boom should jam or fail to function properly during operations, this ladder would offer the firemen in the bucket their only avenue of escape. But it would be dangerous; a sudden contraction of even an inch at the overlapping extension points could easily crush or sever a man's hands or feet. At the side of the escape ladder is the pipe that carries water to the stang gun in the bucket. The stang throws out water with three times the pressure a normal hose ejects. The gun must never be used on an occupied building since such force could push a fire back inside.

It requires constant repetition and practice to operate the tower ladder effectively. The driver is positioned at the pedestal where there are levers that make the boom move from side to side and straight up or down like an elevator. Given the ladder's seventy-five-foot reach, these controls enable the men in the bucket to scan the entire facade of a five- or six-story loft or tenement building and pinpoint the exact location of a fire in moments. Receiving this information via walkie-talkie, the engine officer inside the building can move his hose line directly to the right place, thus saving precious time.

Inside the bucket, there is another control. It is like the stick a helicopter pilot uses to guide his craft. With it, the truck's outside vent man can take charge of all the tower ladder's movements from the man at the pedestal. Now he can maneuver the bucket until it touches the outside of a windowsill. If people are trapped in a burning apartment, they

can climb out through the window right onto the bucket's steel platform and be lowered to the street.

Invaluable as it is in fighting tenement, private home, and loft building fires, the tower ladder has its limitations. New York, like most modern urban centers, has grown *up*. A bad fire on a high floor of a high-rise apartment is the kind of situation every fireman dreads. The possibility of a major conflagration in one of the city's many skyscraper office towers is an even more frightening prospect. Despite the laws requiring that all such buildings be thoroughly fireproofed and sprinklered, the desire to save on construction costs produces many violations. Trying to evacuate thousands of terrified office workers from a burning building is a nightmare. Extensive use of plastic construction materials poses another threat: Some of these plastics release toxic gases when burning. The greatest problem of all lies in the basic design of modern skyscrapers: All of their windows are permanently sealed shut. Fires intensify when they are confined, yet even in the most desperate circumstances firemen dare not break skyscraper windows. Falling from a height of thirty or forty floors above the street, shattered fragments of glass are lethal to all life below.

It is the ladder men who do the bull work at fires. They are the ones who work with the axe, the crowbar, the steel-hooked poles, and the heavy, portable saw. They are the ones who force entry and they are also the ones who rescue most fire victims.

Most of the men in Ladder 9 are over six feet tall and bruisers. Pound for pound, they are no stronger than the men in Engine 33. But more height gives them a better reach when they chop out walls with their axes or pull down ceilings with their hooks. More muscle makes it easier to carry a fire victim out of a burning building.

Ironically, it is the truck men who are usually resented by the public. Some people believe that they cause unnecessary destruction of property. When a truck man saves someone's life, he is a hero. But when people look at the ruins of what was once their home or business, he suddenly becomes a villain. That's why a truck man's favorite expression is, "It ain't easy, pal. It ain't easy."

Lieutenant Eddie Beck is a veteran fireman of more than twenty-four years, many of them spent with Engine 33. Calm and competent, he knows how important it is to instill confidence in his young firefighters. Many years ago, at his first serious fire, he was terrified, almost ready to quit. The officer he was following into a burning building paused and said, "Son, hang on to my coattails.

You're gonna do just fine." And, to his own surprise, he did. "Big" Beck has never forgotten those words.

In a bad fire, the officer will always assign the nozzle position to his most experienced man. Right behind him is the back up man who helps steady the hose, and the third man's job is to keep the line clear of kinks and folds when it is in use.

Generally, the men assigned to duty in an engine company tend to be short and stocky. That's because in a burning building they must work as close to the ground as possible, below the rising level of heat and smoke. It's a lot easier for a short man to work in a crouched position than it is for a tall one. But it takes a tremendous amount of sheer physical strength to control a charged hose line. With the nozzle ejecting fifty to one hundred pounds of water pressure per square inch, it is like trying to hang on to a writhing python. Then, once the line is charged, the nozzle must be made to turn in a circular, clockwise movement at a forty-five-degree angle when it is trained on a fire. This pushes the flames away. (If a *counter*-clockwise movement is employed, the fire roars back on the hose-men.) No one has ever been able to figure out why this happens.

The equipment is subjected to tremendous daily wear and stress, and it is largely the responsibility of the men in every company to maintain their vehicles and to make sure that everything they use is in perfect working condition at all times. Firemen take great pride in their combined mechanical knowledge, experience, and skills. Except for major overhauls, they prefer to analyze a problem

and fix a mechanical defect or malfunction themselves, rather than send their truck or engine to the department's maintenance shops to be repaired. They also take pride in the appearance of their rigs. Even the lettering and decorative work around the truck and engine chassis has been lovingly hand painted in each company.

At four-thirty in the morning, the buzzer goes off three times and the lights come on in the men's bunk room. "Everybody goes!" bellows the man on house watch downstairs.

"Aw, nuts," groans Johnny "Bop." "Give a guy a break, will ya? This dream was just gettin' interesting."

"Come on, get the lead out!" growls Phil "Mr. Congeniality" Weber, tugging his pants on. "What do ya think you're gettin' paid for?"

In seconds, the men are wide awake, their hearts pounding, adrenalin pumping through their bodies as they dress and race toward the fire poles to the apparatus floor.

The streets of the city are eerily silent and empty at this hour, but the men know that they are on their way to a multiple-alarm fire in Greenwich Village.

A dense cloud of black smoke pours onto the street from the basement beneath a boutique. The rest of the building is fully occupied.

"Get everybody out!" a fire chief snaps. It is he who directs the plan of attack. Firemen rush inside to wake the sleeping tenants and help them out of the building.

Two men from Ladder 9 are ordered to break into the basement from the street. When they enter, the place is pitch black. They can't see any flames, but there is intense heat and so much smoke that it is impossible for them to see where they are going. They are forced to crawl toward the source of the heat on their hands and knees, breathing through their Scott masks, probing for obstacles with their hooks. They are joined by men of the Special Rescue Unit. Behind them, three engine men and an officer are cautiously inching in with a hose line. Then, around a partition near the rear of the basement, they are momen-

tarily blinded by the brilliance of the fire devouring stack after stack of neatly piled merchandise.

The engine officer cracks open his face mask and shouts into his walkie-talkie, "Okay, Hank! Give us water!"

Instantly the area is enveloped in a white fog as the water hits the flames.

Outside, the street is now lined with additional firefighting equipment and firemen who are ordered to stand by. People are still being evacuated from the building.

In the basement, once the main body of fire has been knocked down, the Rescue-Unit men move in to separate the burning stock, allowing the water to soak everything more effectively. At the same time, the men from Ladder 9 have discovered a narrow staircase leading up to the boutique. It is enveloped in flames. A second hose line has been stretched inside. The new engine crew attacks this area while the first company concentrates on dousing theirs.

Now the men from Ladder 9 have forced entry into the boutique itself. Here they find flames climbing the walls, threatening the apartment on the floor above. Immediately they begin to chop open the burning walls in order to give the hose men following them easier access to the spreading fire.

For the men inside, time acquires a surreal quality. Their every action seems to be happening in slow motion, but, in fact, they are working like demons. This time they are lucky. By having arrived so quickly on the scene, they succeed in halting the fire's further progress.

An hour and a half later, after extensive overhauling, the men come out onto the street exhausted, covered with grime and soot, their blackened faces giving them the appearance of coal miners. They are greeted with cheers from the evacuated tenants standing huddled under blankets on the sidewalk.

Back in quarters, everyone makes a beeline for the kitchen, where they shed filthy shirts and begin to scrub up at the big sink.

Paulie "Pancakes" fixes a fresh pot of coffee.

"Hey, I'm hungry. You vultures leave anything over from dinner last night?" asks Weber.

"You can have mine, sweetheart," says Johnny "Bop" with a grin. "I'm goin' back to sleep. I just gotta find out what happens next. There I was, sittin' on the sofa next to this gorgeous blond!"

"Yeah, Johnny. *We* know," Weber laughs through a mouthful of cold chicken. "Keep on dreamin'!"

One evening an alarm comes in just as the men are finishing dinner. The fire is in an occupied apartment building just a few blocks away from quarters. A thin ribbon of smoke seeps out from under the building superintendent's apartment. All the windows are nailed shut and have to be pried open to let fresh air into the apartment.

"Fire department! Open up!" roars Ladder 9's lieutenant, pounding on the door with his massive fist. There is no response. "Okay, boys. Break it open."

There is the sound of a sliding bolt and the lock clicks loudly. In the doorway, surrounded by white smoke, is the superintendent, dressed in his underwear. "Wha—? Whassamatta?" he mumbles, rubbing his bloodshot eyes.

The firemen rush inside. On the kitchen stove they find a burning chicken, now reduced to an ember the size of a small apple.

"S—no problem," the man giggles. "Buy another chicken tomorrow."

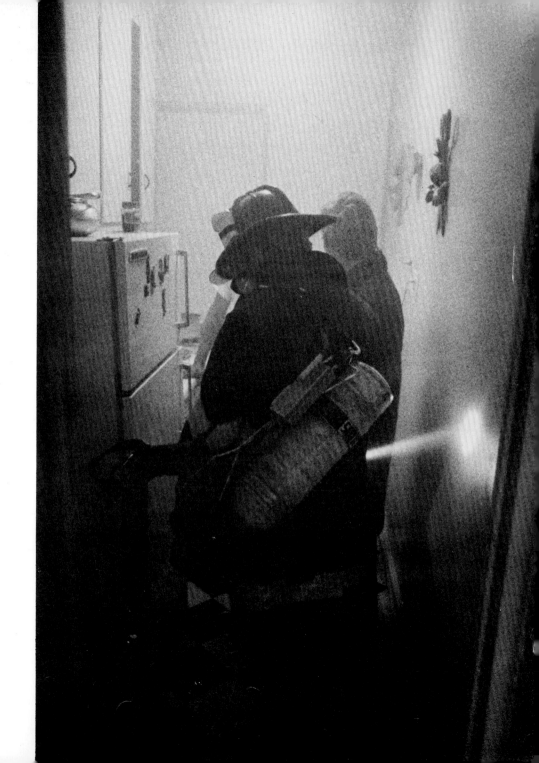

The lieutenant shakes his head in exasperation. More people die from smoke inhalation and suffocation than from flames. "Listen, pal," he advises. "Next time you drink, maybe you better not cook." But he knows his advice is falling on deaf ears.

In between runs and other duties, a man may want to be by himself in a quiet place to smoke a cigarette, read, study for a fire-department exam, or just relax and daydream. Because the city has no funds for firehouse comforts, practically all firehouse furniture has to be provided by the men themselves. Fortunately, firemen are resourceful scavengers, constantly on the lookout for chairs, sofas, tables and odds and ends left out on the street to be carted away in sanitation-department trucks. With some glue, fresh paint or varnish, new fabric and a little elbow grease, these discards are rescued from the garbage and restored to service.

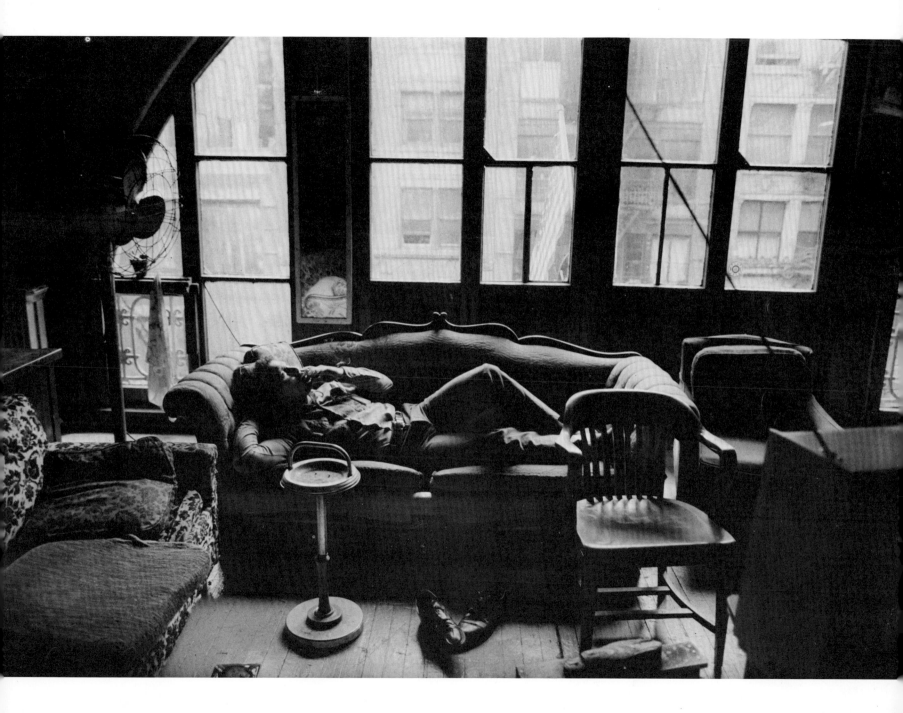

Fireman Andrews is still known as "The Worm," from his younger (and slimmer) days when he could slither through an impossibly small basement window. Assigned to Engine Company 33 in 1963, he has vivid memories of the early days when he first reported to 42 Great Jones Street for duty. There were very few creature comforts in the firehouse. The kitchen was a primitive setup at the rear of the apparatus floor, cramped and inadequately ventilated. The men slept on cots on the building's huge second floor, an open space roughly forty-five by seventy-five feet, with a twenty-foot-high ceiling. The basement was a mess, used mostly to store tools, equipment, and supplies. In the wintertime, everybody froze, no matter how many layers of clothing were worn. In the summertime, no one could stay dry.

The fire department had no funds for improvements, so the men took matters into their own hands. Pooling their time, talent, and resources, they modernized the kitchen and constructed a separate dining room. They built a new bunk room on the second floor that could be easily heated or cooled. They installed additional toilets. The top floor was arranged as an open relaxation area and gradually filled in with salvaged furniture. The building's heating system was improved. New electrical wiring and plumbing were added. The basement was cleaned up, partitioned off, and a recreation room was built, complete with wood-panelled walls. Here too, shower stalls were put in as well as the house's laundry room. Finally, air-conditioning units and TV sets were installed on each floor.

In a firehouse, everybody pitches in. No job is considered too menial or dirty. Fireman Andrews has completed his morning's house chores. The basement floor is clean. Over the years, he has been a big contributor to all of the improvements the men enjoy today. Now, until the next run, The Worm can relax and watch some TV with a clear conscience. He has paid his dues.

It's 11:30 P.M. on a torrid, steamy night when Engine 33's chauffeur hooks up to a fire hydrant half a block away from a burning synagogue on the Lower East Side. Engine Companies 55 and 9 have just stretched lines into the first floor of the synagogue, but even that isn't enough. Engine 55's stang gun has been brought into action, smashing in the bottom front windows in an attempt to vent this level and give the hose men inside additional protection. Nevertheless, by the time the first man from Engine 33 follows his officer through the front door dragging hose, the men can see clearly that it is going to be a dirty job. Engine 33's Lieutenant Russell and his men have been ordered by the fire chief to stretch their line to the second floor, above the main body of the fire. Hearts sinking, the men know they are entering a very old and vulnerable building, and that anything could happen.

Inside, the fire situation is bad. Air

packs are a must. The smoke is so dense and black, no one can see the man in front of him. Flashlights are useless. The level of heat is incredible. Engines 55 and 9 are doing their best to knock the fire down, but it has already reached the second floor. Lieutenant Russell and his men now have the dangerous task of battling their way up the burning, rickety old wooden staircase. As they approach, Engine 9 quickly directs its hose onto the stairs in preparation for the ascent.

The engine company chauffeur is also the motor pump operator (M.P.O.). He wears a walkie-talkie and is in constant communication with his officer inside. He has to know where the men in his company are at all times and must supply them with the water they need instantly and at the right pressure.

Lieutenant Russell tells his M.P.O. to charge his line. Ladder 9 takes a position behind Engine 55 and drops its stabilizers to the ground. Two men climb

into the bucket. In a moment, they are on their way toward the top of the synagogue. Steve Kotchek, the outside vent man, controls the stick. He directs the bucket to the roof where he deposits Pete Brunaes, the roof man, with his tools. Both men wear walkie-talkies.

Another engine company has arrived. They charge their line and, from the street, pour water through the broken bottom windows. Now Engine 55's stang shifts its firing power to the windows of the second floor.

Inside, Engine 33 has fought its way up to the large congregational area on the building's third floor, where the entire altar is in flames. Here the heat and smoke are at their worst. The fire is still rising. Fingers of flame begin licking through the floorboards. Above them, the men can see a large round window containing the Star of David. They are afraid that unless this final level is quickly vented, the whole place may explode at any moment, causing the floor and ceiling to collapse.

Outside, Kotchek has positioned the bucket in front of the circular window. On his way up, he thought it was glass, which could easily be smashed with a few blows. Instead, he finds that it is constructed of plexiglass panels fastened into a wooden frame. He has to rip it out.

Heavy black smoke is pouring through the roof now. Brunaes is in a crucial spot. Working frantically, he forces open every bulkhead and begins cutting large holes in the roof with his portable power saw, creating exits for the trapped heat, gases, and smoke within. Large chunks of plaster and debris fall on the men of Engine 33 working below, but this is the break they have been waiting for. Brunaes and Kotchek have done their jobs well and opened up the intense pressure cooker inside the building. Now, with Engine 55's stang dousing the flames beneath their floor and with the venting accomplished, they have a chance to push the fire out of the building before it can do any more damage.

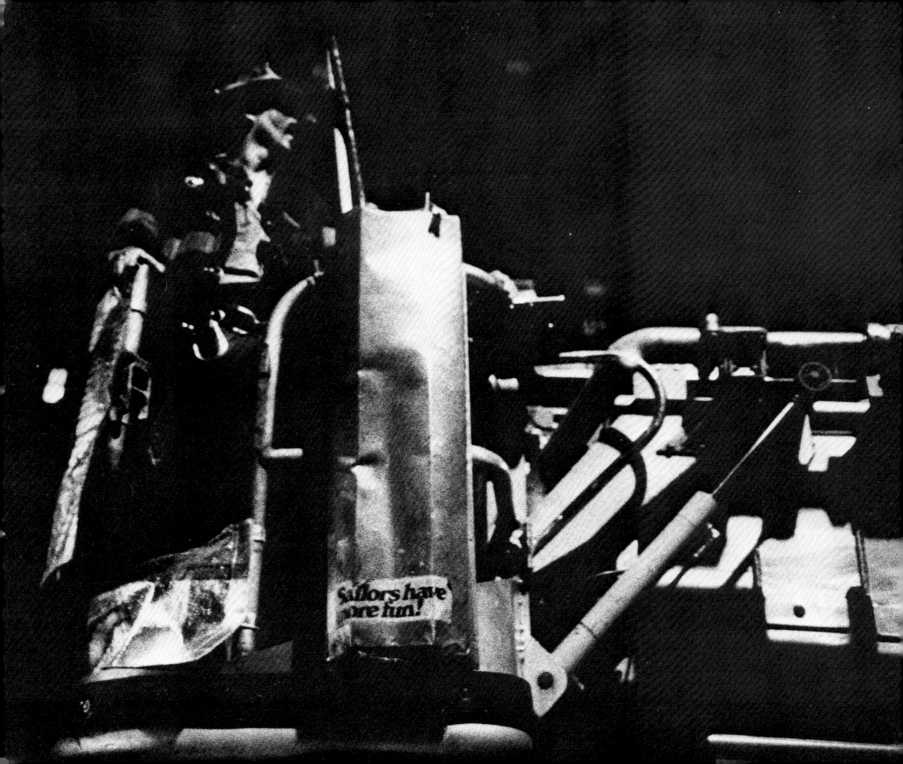

Sailors have
more fun!

Brunaes' job isn't finished yet. He still has to find out if any part of the roof itself is on fire. If so, the flames could ignite the adjacent tenements and escalate into an even more dangerous situation. But after a painstaking search, he is satisfied. The fire is finally coming under control. He removes his Scott air pack, hoists it and his tools into the bucket, and wearily climbs in for the trip down to the street.

A member of the congregation reverently carries the charred remnants of his temple's sacred scrolls, salvaged by the firemen. He will safeguard them temporarily in his home. Then, because they are burned beyond repair, according to Hebraic law they must be buried in a special ceremony.

Only two weeks earlier his synagogue had been aflame. He knows this fire is no accident.

The fire is dead and the synagogue is a shambles. The streets are strewn with miles of hose line which must be uncoupled, drained, recoupled and folded back onto the engines. The men pause occasionally to wipe the burning sweat from their eyes or to light a cigarette as they work together. They've earned their pay tonight.

The house on Great Jones Street has always had a softball team, Bowery U, but it has been a long time since their last championship. For months, they have been slugging it out with the other firehouse teams in their division. Today, having already won a trophy in their own division, Bowery U faces the tough first-place team in another division—Engine 34 and Ladder 1's Hell's Kitchen.

Bowery U is being clobbered. Their opponents have scored six runs in the first inning. Bobby Hemsworth, an outstanding ballplayer, comes up to bat. Hemsworth rips a line drive just past the outstretched first baseman's glove. By the time the outfielder relays the ball, Hemsworth has dived, head first, into home plate. He's safe!

Two runs later, with the bases loaded, the Worm knocks in a three-run triple.

Bowery U has evened the score, but that's where it stays for five more innings. Then, in the top of the seventh and last inning, with one out and a man on second, Hell's Kitchen delivers a hard smash toward first base. Hemsworth plucks the ball out of the air and steps on the bag for one out. Then, whirling, he rifles a throw to his third baseman who now has the threatening runner hung up.

In Bowery U's half of the inning, there are two outs when "Tze, Tze" Mc-Enery, the team's manager, sends in "La Bonz," big Joe Re, to pinch hit. At fifty-three, Re is the oldest man in his firehouse. On his first swing, there is a loud crunch. He tosses his bat aside and stands still, grinning, as the ball sails over the centerfield fence into the East River. The ball game is over and Bowery U has won it.

It's a happy and proud bunch of men who line up for their victory photograph.

July Fourth is a bad day for firemen. So far, Engine 33's night crew has clocked more than twenty runs and the alarms keep coming in.

At midnight, Engine 33 is racing east on Houston Street when the chauffeur hears the siren of a police car. Motioning him to stop, a policeman explains that bedlam has broken out two blocks away on Thompson Street. Three cars are on fire. No engine company may alter its response to an alarm without authorization, so the captain immediately calls central dispatch. Now the dispatcher has to find another available engine company to replace them.

—"Manhattan to Engine 33. You're covered at Avenue A. Proceed to Thompson Street."

The intersection is blocked by a mob. Some have climbed lamp posts for a better view. Traffic is snarled. The three hose men jump off the rigs and, with the help of the police, clear a path for the engine. The crowd reluctantly parts to reveal that the entire street is blanketed by more than a foot of spent fireworks. Large areas are burning fiercely. Teenagers are filling trash cans with fresh fireworks and blowing them up.

The engine shudders violently as one explosion after another rocks the ground. Some of the fireworks have an explosive force equivalent to half a stick of TNT, enough to blow off a man's arm or leg. Several parked cars are burning. The crowds lining the sidewalks, oblivious to danger, begin to boo when Engine 33 moves cautiously forward.

Engine 33's men activate the engine's booster tank in an attempt to save the burning cars and douse other fires springing up nearby. But 500 gallons of water are not enough. No sooner has one fire been doused, when another starts. The engine hooks up to a fire hydrant, and a regular line is stretched.

The first two car fires have been extinguished. The men now warily move their line toward the third burning vehicle, near the far end of the street where a taunting crowd is gathered.

While the car is being doused with water, the captain turns to the crowd. "Now look," he says. "I know it's a holiday, but how about gettin' rid of this stuff before somebody really gets hurt?"

Eyeing one another, the teenagers grudgingly begin dumping fireworks out of the trash cans onto the street, where they are soaked by the hose men. The show is over.

There are times when the men need some way of relieving tension and pressure. On summer evenings, as the night shift enters the firehouse, there are invariably two men lurking on the top floor balcony. One serves as lookout.

Crouched behind the railing, Jimmy Collins watches with anticipation as Leon Pollinger parks his car, strolls unawares onto the sidewalk, and strikes up a conversation with Joe Maggio, who is standing under the protection of the entrance overhang. Collins motions to Jackie "Dogface" Thompson, and together they heave a pitcher of water onto the "Green Man's" head.

"Gottcha, you big ying yang!" Collins laughs, while Pollinger sputters and shakes a fist up at him. But he's not really angry. He knows that even officers will get the same treatment if they're not more alert.

From his vantage point on the top-floor balcony, Thompson spots a man sprawled on his face across the street from the firehouse. Thompson grabs a first-aid kit. He and Collins rush to the man's side. Collins props the man against the side of a parked car. There is a wide, bleeding cut on his forehead. Thompson,

called "Dogface" because he used to be a veterinarian's assistant, probes the wound with gentle fingers and, having swabbed away the blood, finds that the cut isn't nearly as deep as he first thought. Satisfied that the man is all right, Thompson cleans and bandages the wound and helps him to his feet.

Firemen are called upon for a variety of reasons that have nothing to do with fires. The list is extraordinary: blackouts; gas leaks; broken water pipes; violent domestic arguments; stabbings or shootings; muggings; apartment break-ins; delivering babies; rescuing pets. People do not hesitate to come to the firehouse because they know that the men here will give all the help they can.

At 1 A.M. on an unexpectedly cold autumn morning, the men are called to the 28th floor of a luxury apartment building. A sobbing young woman leads the firemen through her smoke-filled apartment to the bedroom where a short circuit in the electric blanket's frayed wiring has ignited the foam rubber mattress. Smoldering, it emits a veil of noxious smoke.

Weber produces a length of rope from his coat pocket. As he and the other

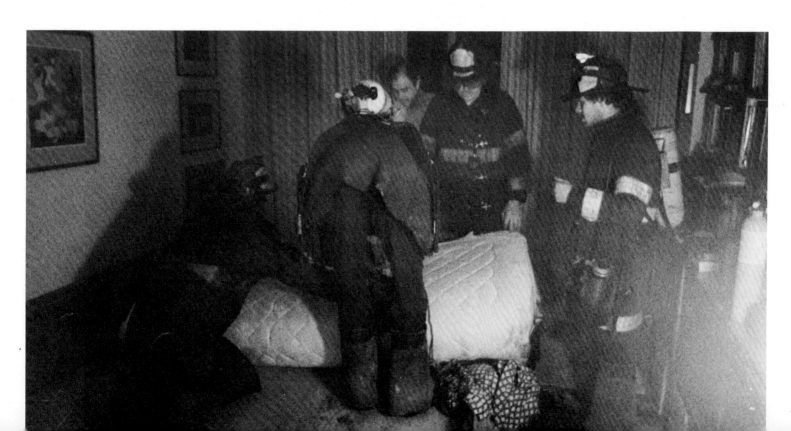

men bend to roll the mattress up and tie it, he catches the woman's nervous glance around the room. "Don't worry." He smiles. "We'll be careful."

The men carry the smoking mattress out into the street where Nick Vadola is standing by with the engine.

"Is this what you guys dragged me outa' bed for?" he complains with a grin. "Let's give this baby a bath and go home."

Vadola unties the mattress and opens up the fire hydrant at the curb. The men watch, shivering, as the water soaks away the last traces of smoke. Winter is not far away.

It's Christmas Eve and the day tour crews have changed into civilian clothes. They decide to go down the street to the Great Jones Café for a few beers. Two hours later, after cautioning the man on house watch to keep his mouth shut, they steal toward the kitchen where the evening meal is being prepared. Bursting in, Johnny Bop lunges for young Davie Smith, while The Worm grabs a startled Jackie Thompson. Crooning, "I'm Dreaming of a White Christmas," he waltzes around the dining room with him.

"Engine only!" The truck crew relaxes.

The engine crew is just about to go out to buy the evening meal when an alarm comes in.

Hank Roebke, the chauffeur, revs up the motor. "Where are we goin'?" he asks.

"Eldridge Street," replies Captain DiBernardo as he climbs into the cab with the alarm printout. "Some joker is always foolin' with that box."

"I dunno," says Roebke, doubtfully. "I got a funny feeling."

Making a sharp left turn onto Houston Street, Roebke peers ahead and gasps, "Brother! We got trouble!"

Even from this distance, the fire is like a beacon against the night sky. Flames are roaring out of the windows of the top three floors and coming through the roof of a building. DiBernardo immediately radios for help.

The fire is at the rear of an abandoned tenement with an open alley on one side. But on the other side, the building butts up against a row of fully occupied tenements. If the men can't get water on the flames quickly, half the street could be set ablaze.

Over the past six months, there have been three major fires in this same building. Now there is a good chance that the building may have been booby trapped.

DiBernardo and his men have to climb four floors to reach the fire. Every step they take is filled with danger. Arsonists frequently remove floor boards and stair treads, replacing them with cardboard or something equally flimsy. In a totally dark building, with only the small flashlight he wears on his helmet, a fireman can't see the difference. Many men have been injured this way.

Back on the street, Roebke knows that his company will have to withdraw from

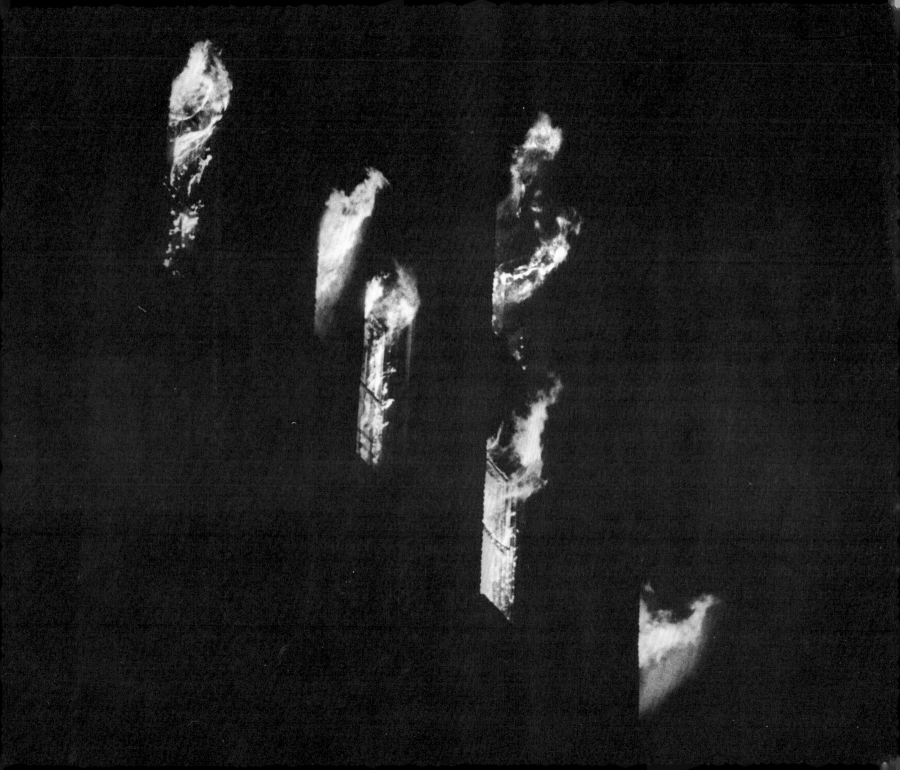

the building unless he can get a steady supply of water to them. With a determined heave, he wrenches off the hydrant cap, which has frozen in the eighteen-degree weather. To his relief, water comes gushing out. This hydrant is frequently vandalized and out of service.

The battalion chief's car appears. He jumps out, straps on his Scott air pack and disappears into the building. Ladder 9 comes thundering down the street,

accompanied by the deputy chief's car. Behind them, Engine 28's crew swarms onto Roebke's hose bed, grabbing lengths of hose. Then, led by their lieutenant, they drag it into the building to join forces with DiBernardo and his men.

"Get the truck into the alley!" orders the deputy chief. "We need that stang!" But there are two problems. First, the street is very narrow, and second, there is a padlocked wire gate blocking the alleyway.

Pollinger shouts, "Cut that lock open fast." Two of the burly truck men dispose of the lock and Pollinger roars through the gate into the alley. He springs out of the cab and turns on the truck's hydraulic systems.

Dick Schultz is the outside vent man. While Pollinger scrambles toward the tower's controls at the pedestal, Schultz climbs into the bucket and readies the stang gun. "Okay, Leon," he says into his walkie-talkie. He is lifted slowly toward the massive wall of fire above.

Flames are burning with the dull red intensity that only diesel fuel produces when ignited. This is a clear case of arson. Engine 33 is moving slowly. If the men can't knock the fire down here, there isn't a chance that they can work their way up through the two remaining fire doors. Burning timbers begin to crash down onto the landing. It is hopeless. The floors above could collapse at any moment.

The men have been working for only fifteen minutes. To them—exhausted, short of breath, suffering from dehydration—it seems like hours.

Schultz has maneuvered the tower's bucket to a standby position about thirty feet away from the building's burning facade. Even at this distance, he has to wait until all the men inside have moved down to a position of safety.

In a sounder building, it would be enough for the men to retreat to one floor below the fire before a tower stang is activated. But in this firetrap, the battalion

chief makes sure that every man gets two floors below the fire level before he tells Ladder 9 that the coast is clear.

Up in the bucket, Schultz knows he can't put the fire out one floor at a time. He's got to build up a cumulative effect and work the stang in a crisscross pattern. The idea is to give each window a quick bath. With his left hand on the control stick, he guides the bucket up on a diagonal path, stops, fires a short blast of water inside, and continues the bucket's ascent to the top floor where he works across, firing into each window in turn before beginning his downward arc.

Enveloped in clouds of smoke, he finds it impossible to aim the gun accurately. Misplaced jets of water ricochet off the wall of the building and cascade over the bucket. Schultz is sopping wet. The wind whipping about him begins to form a glaze of ice on all wet surfaces. All of his concentration is focused on maneuvering the bucket and knocking down as much fire as he can. If he gets off some lucky shots, he may be able to punch holes through interior walls, allowing the stang to penetrate more effectively. But it is an agonizingly slow and frustrating process. As soon as he moves away from a doused window, the flames inside flare up again. After a half-hour's battle, angry white steam begins to hiss out of all the windows. The fire is declared under control. Schultz asks Pollinger to bring him down. He is numb with cold.

Two and a half hours later, the men are finally allowed to return to quarters. It is 11:30 P.M. when everybody sits down to their evening meal of soggy Chinese take-out food. The men are too tired to care that the stuff is tasteless. One by one, they drift off to the bunk room on the second floor. Soon there are only three men still awake, Brunaes, Roebke and Maggio.

Brunaes lights a cigarette and stretches out in his chair. "What's the matter with everybody around here?" he complains. "I feel fresh as a daisy."

"You should," Maggio rags him. "You didn't *do* much."

A moment later, there is a loud snore. Brunaes is out for the count. His burning cigarette dangles perilously above his lap.

Maggio aims a kick at his feet to wake him up, but he is waved off by Roebke. He removes the cigarette and snuffs it out. "Who knows," he adds, with a grin. "This might turn into a busy night yet."

PHOTOGRAPHIC NOTES: It is rare that any photographer is pushed consistently to the technical limits of his craft. This book proved the exception. Imagine trying to photograph a black cat at night in a dark alley without any light. Although this is an extreme example, photographing firefighters during night operations is not far removed. Frequently the streets on which they are working have no street lamps or at best are very dimly lit. In addition, all firemen wear coats that are black and do not reflect light. As a result it was necessary to use the most light-sensitive film available and push-process it to as high a speed as possible without having the images turn too grainy. In spite of this, and in order to get enough shadow detail, most of my exposures had to be made at very slow speeds requiring split second timing and an extremely steady shutter release, as using a tripod was not possible.

Two cameras were used: a Nikon F2 with a 28 mmf 2 Nikkor lens and a Nikon FE with an 85 mmfl.8 Nikkor lens. With the exception of six pictures made on Ilford HP5 film, all the other photographs herein were made on Kodak 2475 Recording Film, exposed and processed to an ASA speed of 3200. Only available light was used, and the average exposure varied from ⅛ to ⅟₃₀ of a second at full aperture. Once more it was Mike Levins, with his usual darkroom wizardry, who prepared these outstanding photographic prints.